D1178645

Self-Portrait

Self-Portrait

Tanka Society of America
2021 Members' Anthology

Michael H. Lester, editor

Tanka Society of America
Pasadena, California

Tanka Society of America
Pasadena, California

ISBN 979-8-4118-1335-7
Copyright © 2022 by the Tanka Society of America

This anthology features poems by members of the Tanka Society of
America in 2021 who chose to submit their work. One poem was
guaranteed inclusion for each member who submitted five tanka.

Cover image created by Gail E. Brooks from a photograph of
a cellophane wrapper using a polarizing filter. Effects added by
Michael H. Lester in Virtual Painter 5.0.

Thank you to Susan Weaver and Michael Dylan Welch
for proofreading.

Layout and design by Michael Dylan Welch.
Poems and prose set in 13/18 and 11/14.5 Garamond Premier Pro.
Headings set in 18/20 Rockwell Extra Bold.

www.tankasocietyofamerica.org

Contents

In Our Own Image

Write what you know. Most beginning writers and poets, whether looking for advice or not, have heard this admonition. Some writers follow this advice religiously, others intentionally defy it, and still others fall somewhere in between. Each of these groups produces its share of successes and failures. Another admonition, carved in stone in ancient Greek, to *know thyself,* would seem like a good place to start if we are to write what we know.

When we write poems about our personal experiences, presenting our observations of nature and human nature, and how we react to them and what they mean to us, we are writing a self-portrait—tiny aspects of ourselves. When taken as a collection, an accumulation of these poems comes to define the poet as much as any autobiography. The tanka in this anthology contain many examples of self-reflection and self-portrait. In fact, one might say that tanka reflects the poet as much as it is a celebration of the natural world and the universe itself.

When reading submissions to make my selections for this anthology, I chose the tanka I liked best from each poet. Sometimes the choice was easy and sometimes it was difficult. After choosing the tanka, which came from 152 poets, I put the poems into broad categories or themes. Most tanka fit easily into themes of nature and human nature, but other poems made it into these categories because they were difficult to classify in other ways. I combined some of the other themes that seemed to work well together mostly because there were not enough of them to make a chapter by themselves, including themes such as celestial objects, dreams, time, love, death, and philosophy.

The focus of this anthology and the book's title is *Self-Portrait*. This is represented by a cover image that may evoke a woman's face and that also illustrates the book's title poem by "rs," chosen for its poetic beauty and soulful self-reflection. In all, as a collection of poems by members of the Tanka Society of America, this book serves, I hope, as a self-portrait of the entire society in 2021.

Michael H. Lester, editor

The Rush of Dreams

I breathe poetry
in and out like a tree
in the dark forest
or a puma in the hills
or a raven high above

Ricardo Bogaert-Alvarez
Denver, Colorado

midnight sky
oh moon can it be
our paths crossing once again
we give each other
poem after poem

patty hardin
Long Beach, Washington

afraid
of her high-pitched screams
during labor
I wait outside, pushing, pushing
five lines into moonlight

Chen-ou Liu
Ajax, Ontario

music, poetry
the sunlit play of poppies
and windblown sails full
a merry song of finches
I find delight in these

william scott galasso
Laguna Woods, California

no more
lace with thread and shuttle
my words
craft poems as delicate
as any piece of tatting

Lenore English
Grand Rapids, Michigan

flying
are two hundred copies
of snow
over the Eurasian continent
from Latvia to Japan

Mari Konno
Fukui, Japan

gift from an old friend
a newly translated Proust
Remembrance of Things Past
my "thank you" note sent promptly
there's no time like the present

Neal Whitman
Pacific Grove, California

where are you from
i answer at times
"from the moon"
like Kaguyahime
i may return there

Giselle Maya
St. Martin de Castillon, France

from umbra
to penumbra
the blood flower moon
slipping out of
Earth's shadow

Helen Ogden
Pacific Grove, California

serpent bearer . . .
forgotten constellation
quiet in the sky
'til the sun passes through
where winter is summer

Pat Geyer
East Brunswick, New Jersey

already
the night sky
is laying a foundation
for stars to shape
an evening shawl

Joanna Ashwell
Barnard Castle, England

papyrus
tells us nothing . . .
pharaoh's ship
sails in the sky
behind the truth

Mariko Kitakubo
Tokyo, Japan

holiday season
the unending neons and noises
but tonight
all madness masked
by the quiet of starlight

Barun Saha
Bangalore, India

an orange seed
holds mysteries
tree, blossoms, fruit
and a dream
of orchards

Mel Goldberg
Ajijic, Mexico

the best part
of waking early—
looking at the clock
seeing what time it is
going back to my dreams

Charles Harmon
Whittier, California

crossing
stone by stone
I pause mid-stream
carried away
by the rush of dreams

Peggy Hale Bilbro
Huntsville, Alabama

in her nightgown
she gazes dreamily inward
the book she'd been reading
faraway like the sailboat
she does not see

Jo Balistreri
Waukesha, Wisconsin

eyes itch with roaming
movement on the wall
a slant of light, a moth flies by
it didn't know
I'd slipped into another world

Linda Conroy
Bellingham, Washington

side by side
the autumn trees
red and green
each aging
at its own pace

Ryland Shengzhi Li
Arlington, Virginia

time travelling
from the nineteenth century
a melody
finds shelter inside
an ebony flute

Maxianne Berger
Outremont, Québec

paging through
well-thumbed art books
my past reappears
and years melt away
like Dali's flaccid watches

Sheila Sondik
Bellingham, Washington

growing old
is a quirky earthquake
moving slowly
my lifelong wife
stands rubble-free

Ray Spitzenberger
East Bernard, Texas

chatter chatter chat
the magpie in my head
open the cage
set it free
there is so little time

Genie Nakano
Gardena, California

every breath
an eternity—
no wonder
it feels like
I've been here forever

Bob Lucky
Viana do Castelo, Portugal

Silver and Indigo

me, me, choose me
the red wing blackbird
flits from rush to rush . . .
girl of my dreams
drifts amidst dancers

David F. Noble
Charlottesville, Virginia

she surfaces
on the moon
i dip my toe
in the water
already out of my depth

Steve Black
Reading, England

a few hours
on an evening bus
jostled from side to side
am i really cut out
for this affair

Matsukaze
Dallas, Texas

that night
you spoke so freely about
love—every inch
of my skin believed yet
self-doubt was left untouched

Michael Morell
Philadelphia, Pennsylvania

a distant memory
of her haunting dark brown eyes
the wind flickers the flame
as I try to read
the instructions to your heart

Laurance Sumners
Lufkin, Texas

missing parts marked
with minus-sign scars
post-hysterectomy
astonished to find me still
woman enough for him

Autumn Noelle Hall
Green Mountain Falls, Colorado

our tango—
in the crook of his arm
head back
hand on his hip
now closer—closer

Marilyn Fleming
Pewaukee, Wisconsin

the breeze
whispers mary louise
peonies sway
under sparkling stars
dancing cheek to cheek

Sigrid (Siggi) Saradunn
Ellsworth, Maine

grass heads quiver
in the slightest breeze
evening walk
recalling the first brush
of your skin against mine

Michelle Brock
Queanbeyan, Australia

leaves crunch
as my lover arrives . . .
the moonlit garden
wrapped in shadows
of silver and indigo

Dawn Bruce
Sydney, Australia

upon us
the deepening shades
of nightfall—
stay my love until
stars yield to sunrise

an'ya
Florence, Oregon

your voice
intimately whispering
in my ear
I hear only my heart
drumming faster

Carol Raisfeld
Atlantic Beach, New York

outside my window
unknown birds
insist it's dawn
and still
no word from you

Anne Benjamin
Sydney, Australia

white moons fall
through blue twilight
she recites the sonnet
how the body loved
the heart's rivers flowed

joyce futa
Altadena, California

morning chill
the fine hairs on his head
tousled and few
he brings me a hot croissant
and cocoa in bed

Claire Vogel Camargo
Austin, Texas

raindrops
tracing her face
like a lover's eye . . .
sea spray freckles the shoreline
with mementos

Elliott Simons
Southborough, Massachusetts

the yellow eye
of water hyacinth . . .
that short moment
when grandma remembers
her lover

Christine L. Villa
North Highlands, California

my hand on her knee,
hers on my shoulder
after a night
of talking
our need to touch

Ken Slaughter
Worcester, Massachusetts

the thunder
of taiko drummers
and two lovers—
why must we quarrel
in such cold weather?

Hazel Hall
Canberra, Australia

bored she leans
on the pub's brick wall
watching her boyfriend
line up behind
the eight ball

Michael Ketchek
Rochester, New York

you love the bagpipes
the music's in your bones
when your babe cries
the sweet sounds that pour
from the marrow of your bones

Jim Chessing
San Ramon, California

short finger swipes
pull weeds from the garden
arguing again
we tell our daughter
he is not the one

Michael Blaine
Seaford, Delaware

One More Thing
to Carry Around

puddle of night
and the silver
of a scoop
that brings what I need—
this cupful of dark

Kat Lehmann
Guilford, Connecticut

Quick Stop coffee
in a styrofoam cup
then, just the radio,
the map, the long dark
highway home

Roger Jones
New Braunfels, Texas

uncle and nephew
weekly talks over snacks
in the prison canteen
a long, hard road
to forgiveness

Susan Weaver
Allentown, Pennsylvania

a lonely cottage
fresh winter ice on the lake
the sun does not shine
spring may not come here again
it's now a year since she left

William Kerr
New York, New York

the cairn we built
is now a pile of rubble . . .
I follow
the outline of a path
to my secret grotto

Dru Philippou
Taos, New Mexico

this film noir of life
black and white streets
in drizzling rain
technicolor strangers
passing me by

John Budan
Newberg, Oregon

another
three-page letter
of beratement
signed
"XOXO Love Dad"

Seren Fargo
Bellingham, Washington

unbearable heat
at home
I pack for Ocean Shore
where I can fly a kite
letting go of my negative qi

Nu Quang
Seattle, Washington

we cool off
in ocean breezes
after
a hot summer
argument

Deborah P Kolodji
Temple City, California

bookstore
I search
for something
to distract me
from myself

Gregory Longenecker
Pasadena, California

Please don't tell me
your secrets—
it would be
one more thing
to carry around

Alexis Rotella
Greensboro, North Carolina

once more
to remember me by
I say no
I want our last time to be
when I didn't know about her

Pris Campbell
Lake Worth, Florida

shattered glass
glistening
in the sunlight
I follow the trail
of the brokenhearted

Jackie Chou
Pico Rivera, California

my sister reveals
she was disappointed
not to marry
the popsicle man
as I had promised

Jeanne Lupton
Berkeley, California

the sunbeams
seep below the cliff
opening up a world—
I should have smoked
fewer cigarettes

Pasquale Asprea
Genoa, Italy

sudden storm
white caps on the lake
our boat
strains at the anchor—
I wish I'd learnt to swim

Keitha Keyes
Sydney, Australia

autumn storm
leaves flash
their silvery undersides—
aging swimmers
at the pool

Ann Corbett Burke
Orefield, Pennsylvania

her smile stands out
in a sea of city faces . . .
the balloon seller
gives the rag-tag child
the red one

Rebecca Drouilhet
Picayune, Mississippi

after four years
i should have known
you weren't serious—
pots and pans
for christmas

Taura Scott
Duarte, California

hot porridge
makes a fevered tongue—
how distasteful
when only quick lime pickle
is available for relief

Radhamani Sarma
Chennai, India

tears in egg flower soup
Fu Yung Lowe closes
cook ready to retire
after 40 years
now too high rent

Janis Albright Lukstein
Rancho Palos Verdes, California

here we are
after fifty-four years—
you, the gardener,
me, the cook rinsing grit
from a bowl of greens

Carole MacRury
Point Roberts, Washington

Drawing Dragonflies

at the bonfire's edge
fireflies winking between
sparks and stars
the child's heavy head
on my bent shoulder

Teri White Carns
Anchorage, Alaska

legs
pink as their shoes
they walk
in the sun
for the first time

Don Miller
Las Cruces, New Mexico

baby-filled day
breakfast on the run
what fueled the hours
before raspberry lips
and kookaburra laughs

Carole Harrison
Jamberoo, Australia

a little girl
sure of her powers
of enchantment
now late spring turned to the summer
of drawing dragonflies

Kath Abela Wilson
Pasadena, California

gripping
the edge of my seat
in the car
my daughter's driving
a little wobbly

Susan Burch
Hagerstown, Maryland

the last leaves
in the wind
are flying away
the whims of the child
locked inside me

Giovanna Restuccia
Modena, Italy

a diva shines
in the spotlight . . .
her other self
hides behind zircons
and a painted smile

Marilyn Humbert
Berowra Heights, Australia

dragons
dance under the new moon
I decide
not to mention their ritual
to my new neighbors

Roberta Beach Jacobson
Indianola, Iowa

grandma sews her quilt
while grandpa tells stories
in the parlor
both embroidering
in their own way

Roy Kindelberger
Edmonds, Washington

I want to sleep
the way my grandfather
once slept
    floating on a northern lake
    his day on pause

Louisa Howerow
London, Ontario

green faeries abound
dancing across the ballroom
they whisper to me
"embrace your inner faery"
as i sip a fresh absinthe

Sarah Turnbull
New York, New York

power outage
suddenly, no white noise
filling the space
birdsong, trees, wind
but humans think our world shifts

Sandra Renew
Canberra, Australia

first impression
reading the tea leaves
I pour another cup
trying to understand
what is not quite said

Barbara Tate
Winchester, Tennessee

an oak tree
casts its shadow on me—
hidden words
are emerging to echo
and reecho within

Aya Yuhki
Tokyo, Japan

a mallard
following its mate
across the pond
how I always seem
to ride in your wake

Bryan Rickert
Belleville, Illinois

Our life
tangled like
earbuds
before the rise
of bluetooth

Seth Kronick
Whittier, California

ancient byway
mud head kachina
in a kiva dream
how serious the need
for silliness

Marilyn Ashbaugh
Edwardsburg, Michigan

at the cat show
my precious Miss Silky Supreme
behaves like a princess
her baby blues blink
to impress the judge

Janet Qually
Memphis, Tennessee

in caves
around the world
art and symbols
on ochre walls . . .
I was here

Susan Constable
Parksville, British Columbia

noticing
her open sketchbook
shrewd glances
oh my god she's drawing me
and I'm writing her

Gerry Jacobson
Canberra, Australia

in my fruit bowl
apples, pears, lemons, grapes
if only
I had the tiniest trace
of Van Gogh in me

Catherine Smith
Sydney, Australia

hometown road
not the same width I sprinted
in childhood—
even the landscape reshaped
where our house was

Lenard Moore
Raleigh, North Carolina

lying in bed,
with frost on the windows
I paint
another self-portrait
in Prussian blue

rs
Middletown, Delaware

In the Maple Boughs

reeds
around the old fishpond
a heron
finds a vantage point
. . . and waits

Margaret Conley
Hunters Hill, Australia

briefly visiting
a downy woodpecker
comes . . . nibbles . . . gone
silent is his approach
silent is my pleasure

Adelaide B. Shaw
Somers, New York

the snow geese
and the dark Canadas
fly together—
their cries
in perfect harmony

Marje A. Dyck
Saskatoon, Saskatchewan

the shadow of birds
adjusting their course . . .
monsoon wind
the change in the sunlight
as I race the storm home

C. William Hinderliter
Phoenix, Arizona

a circle
of goldfinch feathers—
an owl's eyes shut
high up in the maple boughs
with claws hidden in a roost

Paul Cordeiro
Dartmouth, Massachusetts

curve-billed thrasher
builds her nest
in the arms of cane cholla
my own hair
woven in it

Barbara Robidoux
Santa Fe, New Mexico

seems like magic
that some things hover
it's just physics
the impossible blur
of hummingbird wings

J. Shannon Swan
Sudbury, Massachusetts

summer dusk
hummingbirds dip
into monarda for one last sip
while wildfire smoke
tarnishes the moon

Susan Godwin
Madison, Wisconsin

goldfinches
bathing in the backyard
fountain
my second birth
in a marsh pond

Victor Ortiz
Bellingham, Washington

on a nature walk
my shadow merges
with a tree trunk's shadow
a hidden bird
begins to sing

John Rowe
El Cerrito, California

a late cold snap
eggs in a robin's nest
two more in a dove's
children abandoned
lost in the storm

James B. Peters
Cottontown, Tennessee

whipping egg whites
into the lightest foam . . .
I whisper my gratitude
to four brown eggs
still warm from their nest

Mary Kendall
Chapel Hill, North Carolina

asked why
I never moved back
to the city
now I just point
up at the green mountains

John Quinnett
Bryson City, North Carolina

red sun at night
sailor's delight
let someone
explain this
wildfire sky

LeRoy Gorman
Napanee, Ontario

staring
at ashes and rubble
hugging you
with mixed emotions
thankfulness and grief

Robert Erlandson
Birmingham, Michigan

the black storm passes
leaving this
balm of sweet air
an old man walking
past fireflies

David Chandler
Chicago, Illinois

silvereyes swing
on the suspended block
of tallow . . .
watching their antics
I banish winter blues

Elaine Riddell
Hamilton, New Zealand

the flicker of candles
and swaying grasses in the wind
old cemetery
only the gurgling croak
of ravens

Iliyana Stoyanova
St Albans, England

Whistling Wind

into the hammock
fiddlehead ferns unfurl
all around us
our mindful journey
into the moment

Antoinette Libro
Sea Isle City, New Jersey

so many mysteries
in my inherited garden . . .
watching, waiting
until autumn, until I know
everyone's name

Sally Biggar
Topsham, Maine

he snips and wires
every branch
so many blossoms
weigh down
the bonsai trees

> Sharon Lynne Yee
> Torrance, California

wild forsythia
beautiful and unashamed
beckoning
to be touched
just one brief tryst

> David Lee Hill
> Bakersfield, California

the god
of little green things
slipping
down a cattail spike
early morning light

> Jenny Ward Angyal
> Gibsonville, North Carolina

first farmer's market
fresh greens and yellow flowers
fill the church parking lot
we are parishioners
of mother earth today

Mike Stinson
Lincoln, Nebraska

the widow next door . . .
a swing set for the grandkids
in the side yard
and her windowsills filled
with red geraniums

Elinor Pihl Huggett
Lakeville, Indiana

summer days
filled with a long shrilling
of cicadas,
emptied of much-loved voices—
my roses bloom and bloom

Amelia Fielden
Wollongong, Australia

working class
roots and branches
do the heavy work
while leafy crowns dance
in the summer breeze

Rick Jackofsky
Rocky Point, New York

sitting on the shore
observant of the ocean
soaking the sand smooth
the salt-encrusted pines bent
by the wind that whistles through

Cynthia Anne Cashman
Los Angeles, California

it's almost like
last year
give or take one or two
snow flurries
from the Northwest

Mike Montreuil
Ottawa, Ontario

a whipping wind
saddles the afternoon
with self-drawn art
tumbleweeds canter
in sync with the horse

Mary Davila
Buffalo, New York

Shaolin Temple
usually the sounds of
monks
practicing kung fu—
the roar of raging waters

Johnnie Johnson Hafernik
San Francisco, California

in summers to come
when I'm no longer here
who will
set out a bowl of water
for the hedgehog to drink

Ruth Holzer
Herndon, Virginia

seals swim
in the distance
deep sand
soft and forgiving
the way the ancients speak

Xenia Tran
Nairn, Scotland

dipping
and darting
across the pool
a blue dragonfly—
the fog lifts

Joanne Watcyn-Jones
Sydney, Australia

a rusty anchor
heavy chains attached
whispers
of its peripatetic life
to the creatures in the sand

Gail E. Brooks
Laguna Beach, California

1,000 years
the Ginkgo tree grew
by the temple steps
in the trunk with limbs
ripped apart

Carmen Sterba
University Place, Washington

a flash of metal
beneath the asparagus
last year's missing hoe
waiting for discovery
waiting for salvation

michael flanagan
Woodbury, Minnesota

in Kazakhstan
mushroom pickers
wander the high plains
bags tied to their chests
vipers slip through the tulips

Marcyn Del Clements
Claremont, California

trapped
on the wrong side
of our windowpane
a fly's afternoon
misadventure

Madhuri Pillai
Melbourne, Australia

a coyote lopes
off the trail
as I approach
hard to escape
my carbon footprint

David C. Rice
Berkeley, California

a plague
of smokestacks belching
obscenities . . .
on this frosted morning,
even they are beautiful

Debbie Strange
Winnipeg, Manitoba

a coal train
stretching from here
to somewhere
disappears on the horizon
Wyoming

Marc Thompson
Minneapolis, Minnesota

The Wild Moor

my sand-drawn message
taken by the tide
before me
the panpsychism panoply
of a cosmic stone

Vicki Miko
Costa Mesa, California

you are not one,
you are a thousand . . .
by Rumi's hand
the dawnlit willow
in a warbler's song

Claire Everett
Northallerton, England

my baby son
speaks not in tongues
but prelinguistic squeals—
when he learns to talk
he will be less eloquent

Michael Dylan Welch
Sammamish, Washington

perhaps
wisdom has come
with maturity
but oh what I'd give
for a younger pair of legs

Beatrice Yell
Sydney, Australia

A Wiccan witch
a tad delusional
he cast a spell
I awoke next morning
same as I ever was

George Schaefer
Croydon, Pennsylvania

landslide
words known
by heart
reflecting who
I used to be

Cynthia Anderson
Yucca Valley, California

autumn's frosty moon
shines in an indigo sky
a few blades of grass
silver as ice in the wind
melt to winter gold

Jane Stuart
Flatwoods, Kentucky

a yellow ladybug
the first I'd ever seen
meets me at the gate
on my retirement day
great times are ahead

Patricia Wakimoto
Gardena, California

after most of my life
watching others
walk their dogs
here I am
walking mine

Tom Clausen
Ithaca, New York

baby cloud
at the shoulder
of blue hills
the pull of gravity
on a weightless moment

Mira Walker
Canberra, Australia

a toss
of wildflower seeds
to the wind
in life and death
avoiding a fuss

Marianne Paul
Kitchener, Ontario

pink peonies
in our last heart-to-heart
she asks
my thoughts
on life after death

Judith Morrison Schallberger
San Jose, California

when the jasmine
shows its white flowers
this late June
I fan their scent upward
to summon my mother

Kathleen Caster Mace
Niwot, Colorado

safe from prying eyes
he'll soon shutter the windows
of an opaque soul
fly to where the departed go
with no forwarding address

Margaret Van Every
Ajijic, Mexico

a watch
he never wore
what father
left me
when he left

Juan Edgardo De Pascuale
Gambier, Ohio

trilliums blooming
in spring woods
since you died
the comfort of
forest angels

Leslie Bamford
Waterloo, Ontario

I gather the things
beyond my ken
and scatter them
in the gorse and heather
on the wild moor

Joy McCall
Norwich, England

my lantern
is now too heavy
to carry farther—
let me give it to you
for returning home

Michael McClintock
Clovis, California

after her death
an image of the Queen
emblazoned
on the King's Standard
hanging from the castle turret

Michael H. Lester
Los Angeles, California

Contributors

Made in the USA
Columbia, SC
14 February 2022

55988129R00061